A Rabbit Ran

by Rick Kristoff
illustrated by Hector Borlasca

Practice Decodable 20

McGraw Hill Education

Bothell, WA • Chicago, IL • Columbus, OH • New York, NY

MHEonline.com

Send all inquiries to:
McGraw-Hill Education
8787 Orion Place
Columbus, OH 43240

ISBN: 978-0-02-132768-3
MHID: 0-02-132768-8

Printed in China.

8 9 10 11 12 DSS 27 26 25 24 23

A rabbit hid at a rock.

A rabbit ran past Scott's cab.

It ran past Dot's cab.

It ran past Kip.

A rabbit ran up a ramp.

A rabbit did not sit. See it pant!